the

BANDSAW RIOTS

ARLITIA
JONES

winner of the
DOROTHY BRUNSMAN POETRY PRIZE
2001

THE BANDSAW RIOTS

Printed in the United States of America
by Ed's Printing in Chico, California

10 9 8 7 6 5 4 3 2 1

BEAR STAR PRESS
185 Hollow Oak Drive
Cohasset, CA 95973
www.bearstarpress.com

Author photograph by Dan Smith
Book design by Beth Spencer
Cover: *The Slaughtered Ox*, 1655, by Rembrandt van Rijn.
Scala / Art Resource, NY.

The primary typeface used in this book is Galliard BT.
The text was produced in Pagemaker 6.0.

The publisher would like to thank Dorothy Brunsman
for her generous donation of the prize.

ISBN: 0-9657177-7-1
Library of Congress Catalog Card Number: 2001090582

ACKNOWLEDGMENTS

Grateful acknowledgment is made to the following publications, in which these poems originally appeared.

American Jones Building and Maintenance: "Arrival," "Meatwrapper's Lyric"

Doubletake: "Young and Married and Making It"

Hayden's Ferry Review: "Shit Job"

Ice Floe: "The Man Who Lived There"

Manzanita Quarterly: "Poem for Your Hands"

North American Review: "In Praise of Big Mo"

Prairie Schooner: "Wild Game," "Poesis: Eve," "The Coming of the Snow," "Winter Night on the Yentna River"

We Alaskans: "Paint Prayers"

"The Man Who Lived There" also received the Academy of American Poets 1997 College Poetry Prize. "Young and Married and Making It" also placed third in the *Atlantic Monthly*'s 1997 College Writing Contest.

for all of us

Table of Contents

prologue

"*He swears every other word,*" *said the judge.*
"*Judge,*" *said I,* "*that is the way we ignorant working people pray.*"
"*Do you pray that way?*"
"*Yes, judge, when I want an answer quick.*"

Mary Harris "Mother" Jones

JANUARY

Morning is a black wing flaring
at a window feathered with ice
through which there's nothing
to be seen but Anchorage
hunkered under halogen lamps.
Industry stops. Too cold
even to work inside
at Wholesale Tendermeats where
the butchers move like slow bears
dazed in the chill of the cutting room,
white luggers stretched over
bulk of winter coats and longjohns.
At break the coffee in their cups
turns cold before they drink it.
They pass sections of newspaper—
a well-worn currency between them.
I see they're selling health insurance
for pets now, says the bookkeeper
behind the counter, who, at age forty-eight
and uninsured, could finally pay
cash for her first mammogram.
And the butcher scrabbling
his fingers in the candy dish
set out for paying customers swears
These fucking people drive me nuts,
and tells about the border collie
he had when he was a kid. Smacked
by a car, not bad enough to kill it.
I had to hide him under our porch
or my dad would've shot him.
We never heard of a veterinarian.
Says his father worked swing
at the railroad, coupling, un-
coupling the cars. In his house

nothing went to the animals.
Hardly anything to the kids.
In the office black and white
floor tiles tell the lie: wrong and right
remain distinct, one from the other.
It's the cold platform they stand on
every day. Their break
stretches to a half hour and still
they're reluctant to hit it.
With four hours and twenty-six
minutes of light, dark rules
the beginning to every year
and appetite sets the price
for red meat. Out of Nebraska
beef tenders run twelve bucks a pound
when you can get them. For months
Americans have been stockpiling
New Yorks and Tenderloins
to prepare for the barrenness
of a new century. They pay dearly
to avoid hunger, to avoid chicken.
One of the butchers worries
about pipes on the outside wall
of his house. In weather like this
something always busts. Every-
thing shuts down. In her reflection
in the window glass the meat-
wrapper watches herself trying
to breathe warmth into her hands.
You never think it'll come to this.
The kid who once believed
she would fly, vowed
to throw herself to the wind,
is hunched in a chair, conserving
body heat, cold and grouchy
at the thought of getting up.

one

The butcher-boy puts off his killing clothes, or sharpens his knife
      at the stall in the market,
I loiter enjoying his repartee and his shuffle and breakdown.

Walt Whitman
Leaves of Grass

DISCONTENT

We broke morning shift
in time to see Winter
in his white coat stumble
and lose his grip
on the box of frozen sky
he'd been packing on his shoulder.
We saw it go off-balance
and tumble to the ground
where it split open into
a seam of light and sunheat
that wrecked the day
for any kind of cruelty.
The wind he'd honed
all season against the steel
is so dull it won't
even break the skin.
He's been at it too long,
the drudgery of cutting each flake
into myriad forms,
the skilled monotony of creation,
and speculates on a new line
of work. A lot of us talk
about moving on, even
Winter hates his job.
But he's hard to predict
and for the time being
resets his white cap and turns
back to the same ol'. The cold
is a heavy load and all he has
to show is a sore back
from hauling each day
in and out of the freezer,
varicosed legs from standing
long hours on concrete ice.

7

The next time we see Winter
it's at shift's-end, leaning
against a dirty wall
in the backroom of the horizon,
a bad gloom in his eye.
I gotta get outta here, he says.
His lugger is filthy.
He gets to the door
before he remembers
to take it off and wad it
into the laundry bag—
he ain't foolin' anyone—
so on his next shift
it'll come back white again,
starched and clean.

SHIT JOB

The machine sucks
and blows in and out
like a yes-man courting money
and all day you catch
what falls out the other end—
meat Cryovac-ed in shiny plastic
pouches you separate out and stack
on racks—the bright red roasts
and beef steaks, the chops and chops,
the chops, the chops. All day.
This. And the warning sign:
AMPUTATION DANGER!
above the hydraulic knife
that slices the film. You read it
a thousand times every day,
each time your hand knocks
against the plastic guard
protecting it. Read again
and make of it what you can:
GREAT DAMNATION!
DANG! A PERMUTATION
TAMPON AND GUITAR or
PURE MAN ATTAIN GOD and even
NO DAMN PIG TREAT!
Otherwise you'd go nuts
and, god forbid, tell the boss
to fuck himself when
the sarcastic sonofabitch sidles up
real friendly like one of the boys
when you enter the dark of the freezer.
He catches the smirk on your face.
MUTANT DOG!
AMPUTATE GONAD!
GO EAT AN ARMPIT!

Anything to keep from hearing
when he leans into your ear
to remind you: *I'd get
a monkey to do your job,
if I could just keep it
from shittin' on the floor.*

MEATWRAPPER'S LYRIC

Out the corner of my eye I peg her
to be the pretty wife of an important man.
Always, it's ones like her who ask, "How can you
stand the sight of blood?" She watches me
weigh out the three pounds of extra lean ground round
and wipe my hands on my apron to keep
from spoiling the clean white butcher paper
I wrap it in. "You get used to it," I shrug
and think of the blood's aged color—
not that hot red shock of a life leaked out—

more brown and watery as old coffee,
blood dull as engine oil on the cutting room floor
where we've tracked through with our heavy boots.
Thursday night must be *her night* to cook
for husband and two kids. Her recipe, from a magazine,
will clutter her kitchen with forty-eight separate ingredients,
an electric chopper and, I'd bet money, a double boiler.
I smile. Count back change. "It's no big thing.
I wash my hands a lot and when I get home
the kidses dog goes apeshit licking my feet."

WILD GAME

First semester graduate student
with no money left over for books,
I worked with my brother processing wild game
after hours at the shop, after federal
inspectors had made their daily tour.
Through loading dock doors came carcasses
wrapped in old sheets and game bags.
What hunters unloaded from pickup beds
and the trunks of their family cars,
my brother cleaned and butchered, ground together
with suet meat the color of darkest wine.
I wrapped backstraps, ribs and round roasts.
I can tell you exactly what a book costs.
One caribou = two collections of poems:
I bought Carruth and Olds.
Moose, by far the bigger animal, were windfall:
two hardbound anthologies and all of Rich's prose.
The hunt lasted clear through October
and in the end there's always a hunter
with so much meat it'll never all fit
in the chest freezer in his garage
and so he leaves a bit with us.
We let nothing go to waste.
The lean flesh of the wild is delicacy
to two kids raised on domestic beef.
Moose spaghetti and moose stroganoff
on the nights I didn't have class.

PORTRAIT OF A YOUNG BUTCHER

For years he watched his dad break carcass beef,
Just saw along that last rib bone and get under
it with your legs and lift, and braced himself
for the 150 pounds of front quarter neatly separated
from the hind hanging by its hock in the cooler.
He knows how to cut and grind and deal
with brokers. He's thirty this year

and one day he'll take the shop over.
Customers already ask for him—same customers
who remember him as the junior high kid
who carried boxes out to their car trunks.
He's well built. Not tall. Has dark thick hair
after the Italian side. First thing every morning,
white coat pressed and clean from the laundry,
he could pass for a medical intern, until
you see his hands—rough and muscled, cuticles torn
from work. By ten o'clock,

he's bloodied as a field surgeon in mid-shift.
At first, he cut himself a lot. The day
he found out his wife had another man he sliced
his left index finger first knuckle to third
with a boning knife: six stitches and a tetanus shot.
In the meat business the profit margin is thin.
He jokes it'll take a million pork chops
to pay off his new Ford one-ton.
On the saw he can cut 40—maybe 50—chops a minute—
roughly 3,000 an hour—*a whole shitload every day*,
his dad would say. Holding frozen loins to
the rapid blade, his hands go numb.

When he goes home at night he cooks a meal,
pops a beer and watches reruns of *The Simpsons*.
He gardens some, few raspberries and rhubarb.
He deadheads petunias and waters hanging baskets.
In his back bedroom he has an easel set up,
some watercolor paper and brushes. He learned
in high school to paint rivers and mountains.
One night he painted his white and black terrier

sitting next to the pond he dug in his backyard.
It's a good likeness. The light source filters
through birch leaves at the right of the frame.
A wind roughs the pond and the dog, eyes
on the man, has one ear cocked, listening.

BUTCHER'S DAUGHTER

Taped to the cooler door, the day's cutting
list includes: T-bones and chucks,
short ribs and sirloin tips, then
pork chops and pork steak,
ham hocks and shanks. He spends
hours standing in one spot
running primals across the blade
while the bandsaw riots in his ear
like a wasp gone berserk in a jar.
One nick and his fingers would flip
like dice tossed on the stainless tray.
It's a matter of pride and luck
his hands are whole, even so,
scarred as two dogs
that fight for their living.
He's worked this shop twenty-five years,
taught my brother to run the saw,
hired me to wrap meat and
two nights a week sent me
to state university where one day
in class a history professor
came up with this: *Children live the lives*
their parents only dreamed of
and all I could think was
What the hell was it
my dad was dreaming back then?
Back when he was the age
I am now.
                           A daughter
is not rare in her desire
to be something more than she is
and change the course of a history made
from the deeds of an obscure man.

Neither of us picked this
as a life's work and yet we're here
most our lives and the goddamned
saw runs all day, every day,
whines through bone
like it's a piece of balsa, divides
profit from loss, drowns out
the oldies radio and the delivery kid's
blow-by-blow of last night's Cowboys game.
Where the body moves by rote,
the auxiliary mind freewheels.
He figures it'll take twelve 2x6s,
five pounds of nails to add
the deck on the back of the house.
He wonders if the steelhead are running
in the creeks about now and thinks how
in fall the woods begin to look
like a famous painting, maybe
something by Van Gogh who,
he once read in a book I gave him,
lost his faith preaching
to Belgian coal miners, and
at the same time found his art.
Something is always

                    given up.
Is this where the kid comes in
to recover what a parent lost?
On the other side of the cutting room
I'm Saran-ing hamburger, 700 pounds,
one pound at a time (holy fuck!
I'm gonna be here the rest of my life)
and thinking up the lines of a poem
I'll be too tired to write
by the time I get home.
Out the window I can see a magpie,

in its beak a hunk of fat
it probably found in the dumpster.
I watch as the crazy bird
pecks a hole in the dirt
and slips the fat in
like a gardener planting a bulb.
What if my dad had been a gardener?
I'd be growing flowers all day,
my hands black with dirt—and then
I laugh because now the bird
is tamping the ground, rocking
back and forth on its scrawny feet
like a tap dancer—maybe
we were supposed to be dancers, and
I'd be running taps across the concrete
floors. I'd ricochet off walls,
stomp on the table tops—then
the bird flies and I think
no, I'd rather fly. Definitely
rather fly.

two

August 14, 1994: Walking across the tundra I am struck by how many bones—jawbones, leg bones, wishbones—we find scattered across moss. . . . Caribou tracks in the sand, side by side with wolf tracks. Everything is constantly tracked out here.

journal entry, Kongakut Valley
Brooks Range, Alaska

POESIS: EVE

Mountains dark those moments before the sun
crowns over the firmed rim of world,
sound of water falling into water—
thin rill threading pool to pool, each pearled

in the half-light of sky. On this morning
she is the first to rise while the man,
still sleeping beside her, is the first to dream
the names of things: *shrew. crow. bear. salmon.*

She is the only one to see the world
as it is, unknown and unspoken,
each rock a solid cool weight in her hand,
grit of earth rough on her skin, the wind—

distant murmur in trees—and in her throat
a low humming note, the echoing
of what she hears. Her own idea of *wind.*
And the sun, up now above the ring

of mountains, spilling light down steep slopes.
The man, awakened to his burden
of words, rises to look for the woman
and finds her among trees, tapping thin

trunks with a leafed spindling she's pulled free,
clicking her tongue. He says her name then,
a single syllable, exhale of breath
in a long vowel, velvet and thin

through his mouth. And she, having never heard
her name, believes he has discovered
sound of wind combing grass, or the soft
vibrations touched off by light in the world.

THE COMING OF THE SNOW

after Adrienne Rich

means the earth, in supposed sleep
under its white disguise, is free
to take up its working song
without distraction.
The fat bulbs, having gathered
into the blackest heart of themselves
the colors of spring, now wait,
theirs the providence of women
who've stored enough to see them through

I remember a woman
born in Barrow in the year before the bomb
turned the high clouds to tigers that would devour
the land. A new teacher came to her village bringing
a box of crayons. In it were colors she had never seen, growing
with the tundra as she did, the white distances,
the pale sun travelling the horizon
never higher than a runner's torch,
and clear ice chiming in the arctic surf.
From that day, the house she'd drawn in weathered gray
became junglegreen and parrotblue. Her rivers ran tangerine.
More? she asked. Are there more colors?
and *kakotâ suk,* white fox stealing scraps
at the edge of her village, replied in a human voice,
You must imagine more than your own eyes can see

Tonight, under the storm, again, poetry—
flamboyant, vibrant and primary,
common as the dusky down of the sanderling
in camouflage for its life—
I pull you in against the white—
the color of wood, the color of fire,
the light along the rafter—full in my belief
there is more, there is
always more   *for Katherine*

22

PAINT PRAYERS

Late October and wind tumbles
through streets like a man trying to break his fall,
desperate to catch at anything, everything
pulling free in his grasp.
At the corner of 36th and Arctic
plastic letters on the America Rents
sign read:

PAINT
PRAYERS
$19/DAY

Stuck at the red light I have time to ponder
the implications of a missing S: that the wind
is an inspired editor, that prayers today need
the glamour of paint to be noticed,
and that God, nearsighted as a human infant,
will reach for bright colors once he's discovered
his hands, fat round fists he curls around prayers
and shoves in his mouth, dividing our lives
into what can be eaten and what is everything else.

I have so many questions:
What kind of deposit does a person put down
on faith? Is it refundable?
And—hope for less than twenty bucks a day—
how's that compare with the going rate?
Will anybody really see these prayers?
Can I pick my own shades? If so,

I would color the world something different
than it is. I'd offer up

the deep brown of trees rooted in the ground,

dusty white of first snow settled onto asphalt
where cars haven't driven,

or the go-green of a traffic light—momentary right-of-way
against the oncoming.

HARRIS BAY, THREE YEARS LATER

for Dave Mason

1.
Granite cliffs rise from the sea
mottled as backs of gray whales
breaching against a blue sky.
In the trailing current of an island's wake

I anchor on outgoing tide,
weight my line to the bottom and pull
yellowed rockfish struggling in tight
spirals to the surface.

From shore an eagle calls
for its mate with a broken voice.
Sound travels over water
like a flat stone, then sinks.

2.
Eagles return to the same tree
each year, you once told me.
Among branches that gesture
to the clouds, they build their nests,
scrape talons and sharpen beaks
until bright underwood darkens
with scars, indelible grief.

After three years, I still read the article
telling how you died in a Seattle
hospital. Leukemia. Pneumonia.
Your marrow a venom to your own body.
There's a photo of you smiling,
in a life vest, holding a kayak paddle.
You look strong enough to pull the bay.

3.
At Harris Bay glaciers sprawl
across mountains like white seals
hauling out on the rocks. The ice melts,
their bodies return to the sea

and I remember your last wish
to come home. A humpback surfaces
next to the boat, an eruption of water
and breath. He raises his flukes and dives,

leaving a ring of bubbles to trap krill.
I think of you now. Stretching over the bow,
you point to the circle as we wait for the whale
to rise again and swallow the surface.

SHORTEST DAY

Winter Solstice, Anchorage, Alaska

A woman is singing in her kitchen, kneading
    bread, adding flour to her board,
        palming and knuckling

an elastic dough. By 3 p.m., longest night
    thickening,
        a black pudding

setting up along the mountains
    heavy and cold. When it's zero outside,
        the warmest place inside to raise bread

is on top of the dryer. She tumbles
    a load of jeans, the kitchen towels,
        her husband's Carhartts

until her dough doubles and rises
    to a bowl-sized cathedral
        of yeast and sugars.

Between darknesses this day
    comes and goes,
        a crack of light

sudden as the oven door opened
    to reveal the slow golding dome
        of bread, then closed.

FIVE HAIKU FOR WINTER SOLSTICE

1.
Dusk. A woodpecker
needles white birch. Earth's cold spin.
Night ratcheting down.

2.
Bright stars glint and clink,
old war souvenirs duffled
in a low-slung sky.

3.
White chrysanthemums
gravid bloom green supple stem
Lost words. Ghosted breaths.

4.
Frozen earth flashes—
nickeled coin flipped in the air
by the moonthumbed night.

5.
Longest night pivots
like a girl deciding she
will not go that way.

THE MAN WHO LIVED THERE...

1.
Gone. Never heard from again.
Not that we'd heard from him
when he was there (unfriendly
bastard). He built that cabin

in one day—more like a shack—
rough-cut with so many cracks
and gaps you could throw a cat
through the wall anywhere. Looked

like Charles Manson—not all
there. I waved at him once—hell,
he put his head down like he
never even seen me.

Pulled crab pots for a livin' off
Kodiak, out in the Gulf.
Crabbers make good money, but
you couldn't pay me enough

to go out in that water,
winter storms—guys lost over-
board and the captain doesn't
even know it. Gone! Crabbers

don't live long. Probably what
happened to Ol' Manson. Got
tangled in the lines and yanked
off deck—five-hundred-pound pot

pullin' him to the bottom
like a dropped anchor. Nothin'
a guy can do 'less he had
a knife. I'd have knives tucked in

my ass if I ever worked
on a crab boat—chance to cut
yourself loose maybe. Better
that than endin' up fishfood.

Wonder if that's where Manson
ended up? Could be he found
a nicer place. I always
wondered what would make a man

take a bunch of perfectly
good wood and fuck it up like
that. Shack leans more every year.
That guy was a real low life.

2.
He lived his own kind of life.
Alone, stretched out in his loft.
I think he read books all day
till dusk, then, in what was left

of the light, he cooked his dinner.
No electricity, or phones.
He chopped birch for his stove.
From our bay window each morning

I could tell when he stoked
it. Through the trees, twists of smoke
rolling uphill like raw wool
through a comb. What does it take,

I wonder, to make a man
live in a one-room cabin
no bigger than the crab pots
they say he hauled each season—

rusted cages baited with
the one small morsel of truth
a man learns about himself
and throws down into the depths

of an ice-clogged northern sea
(that unknown and murky place
where scavengers pinch, grapple,
and are easily enticed

through the trap door). What sharp-clawed
thing dropped in on him to feed?
It must have been something be-
cause, one day, he disappeared.

No trace. Think his name was Karl,
and I know he liked to walk.
I remember one winter
I came across the small tracks

of a hare zigzagging
a field of snow. They only went
for a few yards before they
stopped at the spot where two wings

brushed the ground. Could be one
night—hungry moon on the wing—
he walked out in the open
under a bright eye honed
                                        and

                                                dropping.

SIGN ON A CABIN IN THE CARIBOU HILLS

This cabin belongs to Eileen Black.
My husband Marvel and I built it
by hand in 1957. Friends
are welcome to use it: Perly and his
gang, Johnny Pete, Mike Klink, Bob Eber-
hard and Bob Jackovik, Diego Ron and
Steve Redmon. George & Maria, Margie
and Marty and the kids if they're along.
Donny Shelikov can come in and
Karl and Tony if he ever comes back.
Ed Greeley, keep out.
        If you're lost and need a place
to get in, you can spend the night. I left
Sanka and dry goods. Help yourself.
Please clean up. Don't attract bears.
Leave it the way you found it—woodpile
stocked and kindling dry. Remember, close
the door tight and leave it unlocked.

SIGN ON ANOTHER CABIN IN NINILCHIK, ALASKA

If you don't smoke,
I won't shit my pants.

WINTER NIGHT ON THE YENTNA RIVER
for my father

If the lives we live depend on the stories we tell,
our story, I think, goes something like this:
Late December and the ambient temperature is -45°F.
Every sound becomes an echo rolling down

the frozen river—ice popping, trees cracking
and the few words we say to one another.
I am in the lead. *It's the only way*, you say, *you're gonna
learn to pick a trail.* We travel by full moon

dogging us over our left shoulders—a bright body loping
along the rim of land, coming through black spruce
and alder like an enormous white bear.
How am I not frightened by its approach?

On this

everything hinges: that it is winter and we are here
in this wilderness where other men bring their sons.
That you are a father unlike other fathers and I am *your* child—
a daughter luckier than most—and by this I mean

in a world that deems the smaller share for the girl
and the hero's portion for the male, you taught me
even what sons are given is not enough. I should ask more
of the journey, that we help each other find the way.

By turns, I follow you and you follow me
and eventually the trail is wide enough for side by side.
Always, there will be wrong turns, the overflow to get around,
pressure ridges to traverse. Our snowmachine headlights

push wedges into nightcold where open leads
appear unexpectedly. We never forget this night.
Looking back now, that remarkable moon
begins as a handful of snow a father squeezes

into a rough ball and hands to his daughter. We roll
it back and forth across wide open snow-laden swamps
gathering layer upon layer until it's so heavy
it takes both of us together, lifting and stretching

to reach the sky, to rock the moon into
place and realign the heavens.

three

However, it was my poverty and not my will that consented
to be beaten. It takes two or three generations to do what I tried
to do in one . . .

Thomas Hardy
Jude the Obscure

INFLUENCE

He'd laugh like hell and break
off bits of Alka Seltzer
so we could foam at the mouth
and rave, two rabid raccoons
under the kitchen table
in fuzzy pajamas with sewed-on feet.
Nights he babysat we never
went to bed, never got tired
trying to ride the bucking bronc
though he could throw us
in three seconds screaming
wildly to the carpet. Then, because
he liked to witness its fantastic
speed, he'd hype the cat
to a frenzy, wind it up
till it turned into a gray tornado
that growled and hissed and
tore along the back of the couch,
glanced off the Magnavox
in its leap to the fireplace where
it disappeared up the chimney, leaving
a startling quiet in the room.
          By this time
he must have finished his garage
where he spent nights taking apart
or putting together his Honda 750.
He'd quit the railroad, quit the paper-
mill to trigger the bolt on the kill floor
at the slaughterhouse. Right about
the time he broke the knuckles
on his right hand smashing
the men's stall door at the bar.
Memory can be as fickle

as that crazy cat that bit
sometimes when I pet it.
You learn to give it space
and in its own time it comes
to you, won't leave you alone,
stretches across your chest
at night, heavy and undeniable.
I can say it aches, but most
the time I'm grateful for the weight
and remember always those nights
we begged for sips of his beer
while he sang to us
ratshit batshit
dirty old twat,
twentynine assholes
tied in a knot
until he got tired
enough to invent a game that called
for him to duct tape our hands
to our feet behind our backs,
lay a dollar bill on the hearth,
and lean back in his chair
to cheer on his little worms
as we inched across the shag
to catch the prize in our mouths.
      By this time
she'd be done with her night class
out at community college and
on her way home, done
with the lesson in balancing
accounts. She was becoming
a bookkeeper, meticulous and money-
smart, rising through the ranks
at the old national bank, rising
into a future sprung

from that moment at night when,
tired as hell, she'd pull her Chevy II
in from the alley, right about the time
my brother and I, determined
to wait up for her, having listened
to both sides of our favorite album—
Robert Service's Yukon ballads—
were *hetched on our heads and*
pumped full of lead, sprawled
at each end of the couch. She'd lay
her head back on the driver seat
and sigh, wanting to sleep right there,
wanting all of this to matter.
Through her windshield
the night sky coined
with millions of unledgered stars,
all the lights still on in the house
and the grey tomcat on the roof,
creosote-blacked paws batting
at the dizzy, light-sick moths.

HELLRAISER

Raise a ruckus, I told those women,
beat pots and pans and rattle your chains.
Enough of coyness. Give 'em hell
and when the bosses tell you go home
you tell 'em Mother Jones gave you a chore to do.
Put your brooms in the air, start to howl
and tell 'em by God you'll clean up
any scab dares cross your line.

Fifteen men died
in that explosion in Arlington. I saw
their bodies hauled up
out of the ground and I looked
in the eyes of those miners' wives
and found desperation, not grief. Miners' wives
can't afford grief, they still got children to feed
and nothing left to them but a handful of scrip and a debt
at the company store. Mother, they cried,
what do we do now? and this is all I knew
to tell them: You fight like hell
till you go to heaven and God willing
that ain't coming yet. And I'll tell you this,
I'd been there the year before and I'm grateful
to say those men died organized. And the next day
the miners came out and Mr. Rockefeller
didn't make a dime off anyone's brokedown back.

Enough of hypocrites! Your men
have breathed black air long enough. Now
the Pinkertons are carrying arms, I said, so you keep
your men busy at home and you go
and you claim their right to see the sun.

It ain't fair they spend the daylight underground
with nothing but the yellow flick of a candle.
You claim your right to your husbands, to wash
the hell off them one day a week. Sisters, I told them,
power is never given, it's always taken.
Rockefeller has no heart, and the poor man
has a mansion of sorrow.

IN THE FAMOUS GARDEN

for Linda McCarriston

The Lady Astor is dying, dropping
      shabby leaves from an ornate trellis.
The American Beauty is a wall of ruined
      blooms browning on the vine.
At the foot of the famous rose the other takes hold:
      the ropy weed wraps and climbs,
rising through the failing structure of its host
      despite the gardener's blood-sworn oath
to kill it. His shears enforce
      a brutal order for the fifth-generation gentle-
man who has lived his whole life looking out
      from a house built inside millions
of flowers. The precious blooms
      wizen and fall, cartwheel on the wind,
catch against curbs like full-color leaflets
      from a busted rally. The nameless, hated weed thrives,
survives to claim its share of history, its share
      of what the fomentary soil can offer.
Relentless weed, it winds itself to the heights
      of the rose, reaches into the sun on the balcony
where, unlovely and uninvited, it opens its strange flowers
      in full view of the window, eye to eye
with the descendants in the house.

THE POPE'S NOSE

Sometimes dinner was a hen divided by ten.
Drumsticks were for Nick and Dickey-Ray,
while Pat and Randy grabbed for thighs,
the two sisters took the wings.
Meaty breast to the liquored father,
meaty breast to the eldest son
who raised the banty hens
and chopped the head each time.
God in heaven and sinners below,
there's hierarchy in everything,
even fried chicken, just enough
to go around on a Melmac platter.
The baby sucked the bones.
The chicken's scrawny back
to the mother of too many, bone
and skin and cartilage connected
to the resolute little thumb of fat
that puckered the old hen's hole.

ARRIVAL

Here it is, close as I can come for now,
but even this ain't the beginning—
family portrait taken
ten years after the Civil War.
Joneses. Scotch-Irish. Man and woman
and their first eight kids.
Eight more after that.

You wouldn't call her a beauty.
Hair pulled back, no lace trimming
her black shirtwaist. Severe.
She showed hardly anything
of herself to the new-fangled
camera eye, no smile
as she held up the white-smocked baby,
her youngest, Harley, namesake
of some lost relative from a lost country
nobody knows anymore.

That's her oldest in the front row,
skinny as a rake, wearing a pair of boots
that look no better than two rocks hollowed out
to fit his feet. In the back row her husband
sitting on the stool, out-of-work miner
starting new in South Carolina, leg stuck out
to one side showing he has on the same damn boots.
Everyone else is barefoot.

She made those boots.
Mother and cobbler to a pack
of round-eyed kids she hoped could make
something of themselves. Shoed them, she did,
all with their own places to go: the housewife,

the roadbuilder, the butcher and baker,
the graveyard caretaker
in a Colorado cow-town, each in turn
signing on for whatever the century
would have to offer: wingtips and the Frigidaire,
free land and the Public Works money,
always the war on foreign soil,

and always the legend of a President
born and raised in a one-room log cabin.
She saw it come true, the slogan hard-heeled through
her mother's heart, marching. *In America, your kids
will have it better than you.*

1972: MOVING TO ALASKA TO OPEN A MEAT SHOP

ALASKA OR BUST
bumper stickers along the Alcan

Outside Whitehorse the truck's front axle blew
apart. Somewhere before the border, over-
loaded, the trailer tongue snapped in two.
We slept in the ditch with mosquitoes and burned
the mangled tires of freight trucks that passed
us going eighty. We were amazed by fireweed.
We ate the flesh of grayling and char and played
card games we'd learned back home where we
would never be anything but the poor kids.
When Hanford shut down, whole town went tits up,
the packinghouse closed. Iowa Beef forced
the mom-and-pops out. But we had hope.
The pipeline workers ate prime rib and filet.
Christ, it rained like a bastard that first day.

RADICAL

for my mother

The cases of whole chickens are on a pallet
clear back in the freezer, under
the evaporators where ice collects

like a smooth clear hide, making
a single block of the entire shipment.
I've come for one case

and beat at the ice-bound mess like a crazy woman
until the box comes loose and my hands
go numb, no more dextrous

than feet. Sometimes I yell out
poems, my cloud breath winding away
in the whirring fans, to keep my mind

off the cold. *I will arise and go
now* ... something something ... *bean rows* ...
The lines get lost. This isn't *the bee-loud glade*.

And I'm not Yeats.
Just a woman hating her job,
freezing her ass off in a meat locker,

a woman who found books early in life
and always came at them like a stray
to a strange hand offering food.

Really meant for me? I took the bait:
One woman in all of *Moby Dick*, scrubbing pots
at the Spouter Inn. To Henry James,

the literature of manners, I was
eavesdropper, maid
behind the door to the magnate's

mahogany room. At coffee break
we fight over the padded chairs
in the office, the cutters and I.

White coat, white apron, hair done up
in a bun, I look like the bride
of the USDA, nothing like a poet

who has anything to say. And I almost
believe it until I think of this:
that my mother, who survived her childhood

hiding in the tall grass out back
until the house fell quiet, didn't
fuck me up

despite every excuse,
the poverty and the anger,
the mother with the knife, the father

drunk and mean on a fifth of anything,
and the nuns who would have her believe
people live the lives they're given

not the lives they choose.
She's proof that's not always true,
I'm proof for what is given:

food on the table and my own clothes to wear,
books on birthdays, so much love and
a crack at something she never had.

In the family business she's teaching me the books
because *a woman should always have something
to fall back on*, and so I balance ledgers,

bring accounts receivables up to date. *Should I die
before I wake, you'll have to know
where the money is,* and in this is her faith

that the daughter will carry on,
finish what the mother leaves undone.
That's how it is with us, work

always on the table, the day's receipts to tally.
She's patient with her poet-girl and curious
sometimes about what goes on in my head.

She caught me reading at the front counter
the day our hometown paper carried the story
of Bella Abzug's death.

Born in Manhattan, 1920, U.S. Congress-
woman and a butcher's daughter like me, she called for
women's worth to be held the same as men's—

how strange to think this radical.
I know I'm worth the men.
What I think of are the women,

the books I read, and the animals I eat—I hope
I'm worthy of them. And the family
that raised me up. My mother asks

Are the invoices done? and I go back
to the 10-key. I know whose daughter I am,
and the woman I'm determined to be.

THE MOTHER TONGUE

As if you weren't the one who raised me, after the YWCA
        reading
you ask me, "Why do all your poems have fuck in them?"

even as other women circle and thank me. They love
the poem about my mother who, as a child, hid in tall grass

to escape the brawl in the house, they love the astonishing
        line,
the way I say it, how in the face of all this, she didn't fuck
        me up, and you

roll your eyes and shake your head as if none of this were
        your doing,
as if you weren't the one who told Mother Superior to go
        ask God

for a fucking T-bone when she turned up her nose at the
        franks you donated;
as if you'd never risen to the full stature of your 5'4" frame
        to announce

to the soap salesman's face, when he questioned your mental
        powers and ability
to run your own shop, he couldn't sell cunts to sailors with
        cash in their pants

after six months at sea. You think I didn't hear you
all those times you told me never marry a man who drinks,
        stay away

from those barroom motherfuckers who think, because they
        got a hard dick,
women are just there as something for them to screw and
        too many kids get born

this way, grow up knowing nobody loves them. This is what
        you would not pass on.
You stand there now, against the mural art on the back wall
        of the museum auditorium

demure and proper as a nun, but far too beautiful, disguised
        as a woman
with nothing to say, and no way to say it, well-cut blazer,
        delicate shoes, straightened hair

shiny as the mink some women wear, the kind who'd never
        look at you. You fool them,
you always do. You smile, bat your eyes, look up like a
        sudden devout, and swear,

"Your father taught you that." Oh Christ, I roll my eyes back
        at you, and proclaim
with your gift of a marked tongue that holds its peace and
        flings its hell:

Only a bitch can raise a bitch. My mother's done it well.

THE APOLOGIST

You never flinch when I come late to bed,
chill on my skin.
I slip in sneaky as a hound through a cracked
door to find you awake, waiting.

Under our quilt your body warms like a banked fire.
You're rubbing my arm
so I know you're listening, focused
as any man who works with his hands, patient
as any man who lives by his faith.

Do you remember telling me how
you set windmills in Nebraska?
You could hold two copper wires,
one in each hand, and pace the ground
until you found the buried waterline.

When you stepped directly over it
the wires crossed of their own will.
I believe you now when you say you can do this,
witch water from the blind ground,
tap the pure stream running deep.

Your hand travels my hip and still
I'm talking it out.
Always something in me wants the world to be
different than it is: a level ground where,
the right tools in our hands,

we have the courage to use them, where together
we find the fountain-head
of what is possible, where the poem, written
for love, is the source of everything.

POEM FOR YOUR HANDS

for d.s.

and then you touch me.
Your fingers
are brown-skinned,
reverent the way they
tip the bones of my hips
like a broad rimmed bowl,

familiar and faithful
as those of the old men in the Badlands,
soot-covered brakemen,
my long-ago uncles
who had their own way of drinking—
hot coffee poured from cups
into saucers to let it cool. Two hands,

they lifted porcelain lip
to their lip and drank
strong Section House joe brewed in the spaces
between trains: their watches synchronized,
their days linked, small cargoes
of warmth and pleasure, spilling
one into
             the other.

SLAUGHTER

This morning, feeding the hens,
she found ice in the water tray,
the meadow grass knocked down with frost,
no song in the air but her husband's ringing
out of the dark in the barn,
a hard long note, slow grind
of the knife against the stone. Then
the great bellering of the ox, the roar
of something deep in the earth rising up
to every well and furrow, every mouth
they had opened on this land.
Then silence,

the windpipe cut. And now
the day's moil of hoisting him up,
taking him apart and bleeding him out
into buckets and pails, bowls from her kitchen.
She reaches, when her husband makes the slit,
into the wet cave of the abdomen
for the offal. Steam rises
from the gut, slicks their skin,
hangs about them, a brief warmth
that dissolves into shadow. She takes
the liver for tonight, takes
the dark heart, the kidneys, the chitterlings
to begin their long soak. A thousand times

she must have led that ox
through the pasture gate, scratched his head
while he mouthed the pockets of her apron
for carrots, watched him fatten,
faithful in her calling to turn profit

from what would otherwise only be death.
She takes the feet and tongue, drops an ear
to the dog. When her husband
smacks her rump with the tail
she laughs and he chases her into the house.
Tonight he'll be a rich man with
three hundred pounds to market.

The carcass cools in the barn and the ground
freezes, pulling the cold down, layer by layer
past the husks and dormant roots.
Tomorrow they will finish the breakdown.
Tonight the room where they are is a lamp, a fire
in the hearth burns with the sound
of rustling silk. She chops the tail
to stew for the children. For a while later
they'll be out of her way,
working over the vertebrae,
sucking the soft bones, faces and fists
shiny with light and marrow.

YOUNG AND MARRIED AND MAKING IT
for my parents

He took the job cutting meat to get off graveyard
in the pulp room at Boise Cascade where ten-year men
dealt five-card all night, grew thick in their bodies and hard

of hearing. Early twenties with no particular
gift for parceling a cow to profit, he learned quick
to handle a knife and bone-out a hindquarter.

And he learned quick there are things a man gets paid to do
because nobody else wants to do them. His apron
smeared with fat and pork blood that soaked through

his white lugger to ruin whatever shirt he had on.
His wife scoured them with salt, but never got that dark
spot where blood had leached to come out of cotton.

She bleached them, boiled them. Nothing worked. After a while
the stains took on the look of flowers, faded layer
on layer. She'd give up finally, throw the shirts out when

she couldn't stand them anymore. Nothing
in her life yet had been that permanent. Her body—
even it seemed to change daily, always becoming

someone she hadn't been the day before: a woman
not afraid to touch a man's skin, determined wife papering
her own kitchen, and the pretty bank teller swollen

with child counting people's money at the drive-up
window. She took time off—three weeks—to have the baby.
It seemed so easy, making a life. She washed diapers

and hung them outside to dry until her whole back yard
bannered white and alive in the wind, as if to say:
here lives a woman who will never let another

dismiss what she's made. She was so happy
to be young and married to a husband home from work every night
when he was supposed to be. He'd sit, hold the baby in his lap,

and marvel at her size, her hunger. Things seemed so natural
to him, like the sound his knife made some days
prying through the hip-joint of a hog, pop of cartilage

telegraphing up his arm, reminding him he was cutting
something that was once blooded, once clocked by a heart
no bigger than his own. He liked the work. He was good at the living.

epilogue

IN PRAISE OF BIG MO

In all the commotion, freight trucks
backing up to overhead doors
that roll open with a tin thunder,
the pallet jack's hydraulic sigh and
the fan-driven ice storm of the walk-in freezers,

to stand on this loading dock in a northern winter,
among delivery drivers, brothers and butchers,
among the cases of frozen meat stacked shoulder-high,
our breath rising smoky as engine exhaust,

on the exact spot where the concrete
is cracked in the outline of a scary tree,
and feel the sudden heat billowing
from that big Modine
when it finally kicks on, is bliss.

Gas furnace hung in the rafters,
200,000 BTUs, Big Mo breathes down on us
like a dragon, fluffs our hair,
dries our eyes, loopdeloops invoices
into the air with hot guff, fills every inch
of the receiving room with a foreign heat.

We sign off on the bills of lading
and turn to face him, raise our arms even,
and bask, grateful as buzzards
who first invented this pose
out in the cold dawn of the desert

when the sun finally opened
his great lizard eye to look on them.

ABOUT THE AUTHOR

Arlitia Jones was born in Pasco, Washington, but moved with her family to Anchorage, Alaska, when she was seven. Her parents opened a wholesale butcher shop, teaching the trade to Jones and her brother as soon as they were old enough to help out, and she works there fulltime as a meat-wrapper and bookkeeper. In 1995, Jones received an MFA in poetry from the University of Alaska Anchorage, where she teaches creative writing part-time. Runner-up in the *Atlantic Monthly*'s college writing contest, and recipient of the American Academy of Poets College Poetry Prize, Jones has had work published in *Prairie Schooner*, *Hayden's Ferry Review*, *American Jones Building and Maintenance*, *Doubletake*, and elsewhere. She and her husband Dan Smith live in Anchorage but spend as much time as they can at the cabin they built by hand in Ninilchik.